The Maya

NAIDA KIRKPATRICK

Heinemann Library
Chicago, Illinois

© 2003 Heinemann Library
a division of Reed Elsevier Inc.
Chicago, Illinois

Customer Service 888-454-2279
Visit our website at www.heinemannlibrary.com

Map illustrations by John Fleck
Color illustrations by Marty Martinez
Photo research by Amor Montes de Oca
Printed and bound in the United States by Lake Book Manufacturing, Inc.

07 06 05 04 03
10 9 8 7 6 5 4 3 2 1

Library of Congress Cataloging-in-Publication Data
Kirkpatrick, Naida.
  The Maya / Naida Kirkpatrick.
     p. cm. -- (Understanding people in the past)
Summary: Shows how the ancient Mayan people lived by describing their
social, economic, political, religious, and cultural life, and looks at
how archaeologists learn about ancient civilizations.
Includes bibliographical references and index.
  ISBN 1-4034-0386-4 (HC); 1-4034-0606-5 (Pbk.)
  1. Mayas--Antiquities--Juvenile literature. 2. Central
America--Antiquities--Juvenile literature. 3.
Mexico--Antiquities--Juvenile literature. [1. Mayas--Antiquities. 2.
Indians of Central America--Antiquities. 3. Archaeology. 4. Central
America--Antiquities. 5. Mexico--Antiquities.] I. Title. II. Series.
  F1435 .K567 2002
  972.81'016--dc21
                              2002002346

Acknowledgments
The author and publisher are grateful to the following for permission to reproduce copyright material:
Title page, p. 13B Victor R. Boswell, Jr./National Geographic Image Collection; pp. 5, 13T Craig Lovell; pp. 6A, 7, 20 Werner Forman Archive/Art Resource; pp. 6B, 11B, 26, 37, 48 Kenneth Garrett/National Geographic Image Collection; p. 8 Essex University/Trip; pp. 9T, 14 Scala/Art Resource; pp. 9B, 18 George Mobley/National Geographic Image Collection; p. 10 Andrew Rakoczy/Bruce Coleman Inc.; pp. 11T, 32 Graeme Teague; p. 13B Victor R. Boswell, Jr./National Geographic Image Collection; pp. 15, 29 M. Timothy O'Keefe/Bruce Coleman Inc.; p. 16 Ken Lucas/Visuals Unlimited; p. 19T John Elk III/Bruce Coleman Inc.; p. 19B SEF/Art Resource; p. 21 Hulton Archive/Getty Images; p. 22 David Harvey/National Geographic Image Collection; p. 23 C. Parker/Trip; p. 24 Charles Henneghien/Bruce Coleman, Inc.; p. 25 Keith Gunnar/Bruce Coleman Inc.; p. 27 Humann/gtphoto; pp. 28, 33 Macduff Everton/Corbis; p. 30T Joann Pecoraro/Foodpix; p. 30B Denny Kaltreider; p. 31 Mark S. Skalny/Visuals Unlimited; pp. 34, 35, 45B, 46 Peter E. Spier/National Geographic Image Collection; p. 36T Janis Burger/Bruce Coleman Inc.; p. 36B H. Rogers/Trip; pp. 38T, 42 Danielle Gustafson/Art Resource; p. 38B M. P. L. Fogden/Bruce Coleman Inc.; p. 39 Nik Wheeler/Corbis; p. 41T Craig Lovell/Corbis; p. 41B Danny Lehman/Corbis; p. 43T Lee Foster/Bruce Coleman Inc.; p. 43B Andrew Rakoczy/Art Resource; p. 44T Otis Imboden/National Geography Image Collection; p. 44B Victor R. Boswell, Jr./National Geographic Image Collection; p. 45T Werner Forman Archive/Art Resource; p. 47 Macduff Everton; p. 49 Miguel L. Fairbanks; p. 50 Kimbell Art Museum/Corbis; p. 51 Victor R. Boswell, Jr./National Geographic Image Collection; p. 52 C. C. Lockwood/Bruce Coleman Inc.; p. 53T Ronald F. Thomas/Bruce Coleman Inc.; p. 53B George F. Mobley/National Geographic Image Collection; p. 55 Archivo Iconografico, S. A./Corbis; p. 56 G Howe/Trip; p. 57 Sean Sprague/Mexicolore/The Bridgeman Art Library, New York; p. 58 S. Murphy L.; p. 59 Michel Freeman/Corbis

Cover photograph: C. Parker/Trip

Some words are shown in bold, **like this.** You can find out what they mean by looking in the glossary.

Contents

Who Were the Maya?

The Maya civilization developed gradually from a group of wandering hunters to a people who settled and began to grow crops. The Maya came to the area that is now Guatemala in about 800 B.C.E. The culture reached its height between 250 and 900 C.E. This was not a single empire. The Maya built many great **city-states,** each with its own ruler.

The area in which the Maya lived is split into the southern highlands and the northern highlands. The highest mountains are between 7,500 and 10,000 feet (2,286 and 3,048 meters). Here, the temperatures average below 60°F (16°C). In the lowlands, the temperature is hot

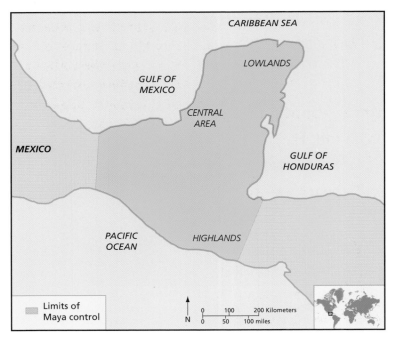

The Maya lived in the part of Central America known as the Yucatán Peninsula. It includes Guatemala, eastern Mexico, Honduras, Belize, and El Salvador.

and there is a lot of rain. There is about 80 to 120 inches (203 to 305 centimeters) of rain a year. Some areas have earthquakes.

Maya people

The average Maya male stood about five feet (1.5 m), four inches (12.7 cm) tall. He had black hair, a round face, and slightly almond shaped eyes. The Maya were a warlike people that used sophisticated agricultural techniques. Their gods were very important to them. They worshiped many gods. To honor these gods, they built grand **temples.** Everything each Maya did was done to satisfy the gods.

The descendants of the Maya still live in the Yucatán. These present-day Maya closely resemble their ancestors. About four million descendants of the Maya speak the Mayan language.

How Do We Know About the Maya?

Uncovering the past

We learn about ancient civilizations from the work of many specialists. **Archaeologists** study the remains left by ancient people. Items that are small enough to be moved are called **artifacts**. Artifacts can be pottery, and parts of tools or weapons. Archaeologists also study large features such as roads, buildings, **temples,** and palaces.

Other specialists called **epigraphists** study ancient writings. **Art historians** study the paintings and different carvings left by ancient people. There are also specialists who study such things as ancient pollen and bones.

This stone disc with relief design shows a ball player. Around the edges are a series of dates including day and 20-day period signs.

In this stone carving, First Dawn is receiving a baton from the dynasty's founder, Sun-eyed Green Quetzal Macaw.

This funeral mask was found in the tomb of a noble buried around 527 C.E. The mask is made of jade, pyrite, and shell.

Archaeologists can discover a lot about a person and their culture by looking in their tomb. For example, archaeologists recently excavated a Mayan tomb containing the skeleton of a man. They could tell the age of the man at his death by studying bone fragments. He was about 35 to 40 years old. There were no signs of arthritis or any hard work. Thus, archaeologists determined that this man was a **noble.** Pots inside the tomb held pigment, and there were many ornaments. It was decided that this tomb was that of a royal **scribe** and son of Copán's greatest king, Smoke Imix.

Writing and books

The Maya wrote in **hieroglyphics.** This is a system of writing that uses a combination of symbols that represent sounds or entire ideas. Many records were kept on large stone monuments called **stelae.** These were used to record important dates and great events in the lives of the rulers and their families.

The Maya made books, or **codices,** of paper from fig tree bark. Codices could contain astronomical tables, information about religious ceremonies, and calendars showing

The Madrid Codex is a book made of bark paper. It is one of the three or four surviving Maya books. It unfolds like a screen to a length of 22 feet (6.7 meters).

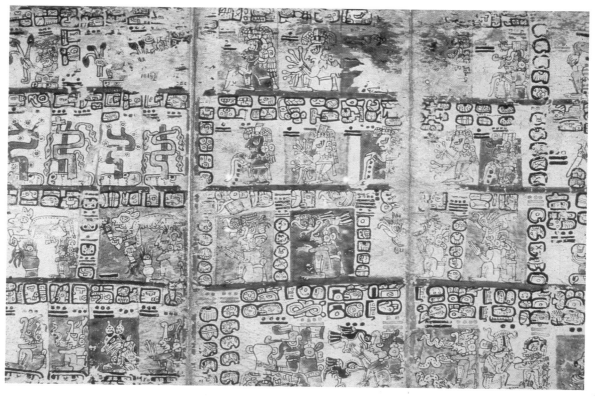

lucky days for farming and hunting. Only a few books from the 1100s to 1500s have survived. Most of the books were destroyed by Spanish invaders.

Maya math

The Maya developed the concept of zero. Their system of mathematics was based on 20 instead of 100, as in the decimal system. They predicted the eclipses of sun, moon, and the orbit of the planet Venus. The Maya studied Venus because they considered it to be the war star.

This vase is made of pottery and stands eight inches (twenty cm) tall. It records a story that can be read like a codex.

These **glyphs** on the mural show two of the four cardinal directions. The rear wall shows east and its association with the sun. On the right is south and Venus.

9

Writing

The Maya developed a complex system of writing. There are **inscriptions** on stone monuments, buildings, and **artifacts** as well as three or four surviving Maya books, or **codices.** The Maya kept detailed histories. By recording rainy and dry seasons, they could tell when it was the best time to plant crops. They developed calendars from the records of the movement of the stars. This helped them determine when ceremonies should be held or when a war should be fought.

Numbers and symbols

Their writing system used standard symbols for several kinds of information. They used a **vigesimal** numbering system, based on the number twenty. The symbols used were dots and bars. To record information not made up

This is an inscription of numbers. The number three is represented by three dots. Place two bars underneath and it becomes thirteen.

of numbers, symbols called **glyphs** were used. Some glyphs represented an entire word, much like the "&" we use for the word "and."

Keeping records

Most of the surviving records of the Maya **script** are carved or painted on stone or pottery. The most important records were kept in codices. These books were made of paper made from the inner bark of a tree. The bark paper was coated with a smooth white surface made of fine lime plaster. The text and drawings were painted on with a brush. The pages were joined, then folded within covers of wood or jaguar skin. They opened up like a small folding screen. Some were as long as twenty feet (six meters). The bark paper did not last as well as stone, and many of the books decayed in the damp, tropical climate.

When the Spaniards came in the 1500s, the Maya writing ended. Spanish church and civil officials considered it to be pagan, and did everything they could to stamp it out. Maya **scribes** were taught European script. The European script was more efficient and soon the ancient Maya writing disappeared.

This is a statuette of a Maya scribe.

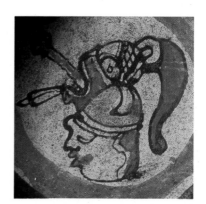

The image painted on this pottery bowl shows a man wearing a headdress. It is the face of the patron god of scribes. Note the two brushes in the god's mouth. This bowl was found in the tomb of a scribe.

Building a Civilization

Settlements along the Pacific coast developed from about 1500 to 1000 B.C.E. People still hunted, but they began to farm to provide enough food. Along the coast of the Caribbean, the same process was happening. Maya settlements slowly reached inland along the rivers.

Not an empire

The Maya probably migrated into the lowlands

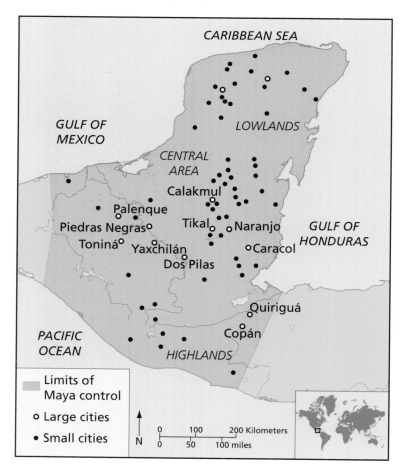

Maya cities were spread throughout the Yucatán Peninsula. Most cities were fairly close to each other, making trade more convenient.

The first ruler of the Copán Dynasty was Quetzal Macaw.

of Peten and Yucatán around 900 B.C.E. There was war and dynasties but it was not an "empire." In the period of 400 B.C.E. to 250 C.E., the first **city-state** arose. Large structures were built. Cities grew and different classes of society emerged.

At the top of society were the **nobles.** Nobles owned land and held political offices. They also were sometimes warriors, wealthy farmers, or clergy. Merchants were sometimes identified as noblemen, but were usually considered to be lower class. Their status in society was determined by the quantity of their wealth. Commoners sometimes owned small areas of land for farming. They could work the lands of the nobles. They also became artisans. Slaves were the lowest members of society. Most slaves were prisoners-of-war or were children of a slave.

To make this jar, each polished piece of jade was drilled, then glued and pegged onto a wooden cylinder. A tiny jade plug covered each nail.

Maya Government

City-states

The Maya civilization was never unified. Instead, it was divided into many independent **city-states.** Each city-state had its own ruler. Some city-states had social and economic ties. Sometimes marriage arrangements were made between communities in order to gain allies.

Still, many battles were fought. Raiding was carried out to increase the wealth and power of the winner. There were also religious meanings to war. The timing and the success of the war was determined by the gods.

Records of events, such as war and rituals, were carved on monuments. They tell about the taking of sacrificial captives from neighbors. This was seen as a mark of prestige for royals.

Maya kings

Each city-state had a capital where the king, his court, and the advisory council lived. This changed due to the success of the king. A major ruler had to be a successful warrior, a good diplomat, and conduct ceremonies as a religious leader. If a king failed, the kingdom

This **stucco** head was found in the tomb of a much-loved ruler, K'inich Janaab'Pakal—also known as Pacal the Great. Pacal became king at the age of twelve and ruled for many years.

failed, too. If he was defeated in battle, his entire region was under control of the conqueror.

The elite council

When the royal order failed, a new system, the *multepal*, or elite council, was formed. This system was more responsive and flexible than the old one. For example, it allowed the city-state of Chichén Itzá to control more territory than its earlier rulers.

A new system

By the time the Spanish came in the early 1500s, there were many governments throughout the Maya region. Some were *multepal,* some had single rulers, and others were just a loose confederation of towns.

Located in the Grand Plaza below the **Acropolis** in Copán is this **stela**. It holds the recorded history of Maya rulers.

Women's role

Women were also important to the Maya government. If a king had no sons, his daughter would become queen. She would rule until her son was old enough to become ruler.

What Did the Maya Believe?

The Maya believed that all things were part of a single existence. They believed the earth was the back of a huge turtle that swam in the sea. The mountains were the ridges of the turtle's back. The universe was made up of the earth, where people lived, the sky, where **deities** lived, and **Xibalba,** where the underworld deities lived. In the center of the world was the great sacred tree of life that supported the sky. East was where the sun was born each day, and West was where the sun died. North was straight up and South was straight down.

Why sacrifice?

The Maya believed the people of the present world were created out of maize. They believed in life after death. They had many gods. The Maya believed the gods needed human blood to function favorably. This usually called for sacrifice. They believed this made the gods happy.

Caves

There are many caves throughout the Maya region. These caves were thought to be entrances to Xibalba and were evil places. The doorways in some of the Maya **temples** were symbols for cave entrances where the kings and priests could enter and talk with the lords of Xibalba.

The Maya believed that Kinnich Ahaw, the sun god, became a jaguar at night. Yax Balam the Jaguar was their name for the sun of the underworld.

Some Maya gods

Itzamna was the creator of the universe. He was shown as a serpent with two heads. One head faced east toward the rising sun, the other head faced west toward night. Chac, the rain god was very important because he nourished the fields and made life possible. Ek Chuah, "black scorpion," was the god of merchants. He was usually shown carrying a bundle on his back. He was also the god of **cacao,** one of the most important crops traded by Maya merchants.

The Maya believed there was no real division between the world of the living and the world of the dead. They believed the dead simply moved from one level of being to another, and could still show themselves to the living if they wanted.

Ceremonies and Temples

The Maya built enormous pyramid-like **temples.** In one, the temple in Palenque, the person in charge of the excavation noticed round holes in a slab set into the floor. When the slab was moved, there was a secret passage. It took four years to clear the passage that led to the center of the pyramid. At the bottom were five skeletons. When a panel of the wall was removed, the excavation team found several **stucco** figures and a **sarcophagus.** This was the tomb of Pacal, a ruler who died in 683 C.E.

This figurine stands four inches (ten cm) tall and was used as a whistle. It may have been used in religious ceremonies.

Special ceremonies

The Maya had many ceremonies in order to keep the gods happy. When something went wrong, such as a drought, they thought it was because the gods were angry.

Ceremonies followed a special pattern. There were specific rituals to expel evil power. There was special music, processions, incense, and offerings. These followed a period of fasting that symbolized purification.

Offerings

Offerings were a part of each person's daily life. A mother might offer a bit of food to the god Ixchel for the health of her child. A farmer

The Great Jaguar Temple at Tikal is almost 230 feet (70 meters) high, with steep terraces and stairs that lead to the temple at the top.

might say a quick prayer to the god Chac before he began his day in the fields.

Sacrifices

As with other cultures, some sacrifices used live animals. Sometimes a person became the sacrifice. The priests would remove the person's heart as a gift to the gods.

Music

Trumpets made from conch shells, and whistles, **ocarinas,** and flutes made from fired clay or wood provided music for a procession of priests. This music was accompanied by wooden drums made from hollowed-out logs, turtle shell drums, bone raspers, and gourd rattles.

The Temple of Warriors is in the Maya city of Chichén Itzá. The sides are 65.5 feet (20 m) long. It is on a pyramid with steps at a height of 37 feet (11 m). Broad stairs lead to the temple. At one time, the rows of columns were covered with a roof. In the Maya culture, only the priest could enter the temple.

The Maya Calendar

Keeping track of time

The Maya called the sun, moon, and planets the sky **deities.** They observed and recorded the movements of the objects in the sky accurately, but they did not understand them. They believed the entire universe was ruled by supernatural forces.

They had several calendars. Two of them form the basis for our modern 365-day calendar and our 30-day month. Other calendars use the sun's cycle to create a solar calendar and the moon's cycle to create a lunar calendar. The Maya also recorded the movements of Mars, Venus, and Jupiter. They kept count of the days with the "dot" and "bar" system.

The calendar of 365 days, known as *haab,* was based on the orbit of the earth around the sun. The days, or *winal,* were divided into eighteen months of twenty days each and five days at the end of the year. These last five days, called *uayeb,* were considered very unlucky. During these days, many sacrifices were made and unnecessary work avoided. The days were named for gods or goddesses.

The Maya recorded longer cycles of time. The most famous is the Long Count. Long Count dates were used by kings to record the events of their reigns. Long Count dates were exact, but they took up a lot of space. Sometimes, more than ten **glyphs** were needed.

The Maya used what is called the "count of days," a sacred **almanac** that repeated every 260 days. One of the uses of this was to determine the destiny of each person's life. Each person's destiny was determined by the patron deities of their birth date.

The Maya believed the number and days in their calendar was a procession of gods who marched along an eternal trail with no beginning and no end. Along that trail were stations. There was one for each day, and others to mark the end of every period.

This Maya calendar shows the names of the months and days, along with the deities associated with each.

Medicine and Healing

Power to heal

The Maya believed sickness, afflictions, and death were the result of wrongful living and sins. Physicians performed their cures by bleeding the parts of the body that hurt. In addition to physicians, there were traditional healers called **shamans.**

A shaman was called upon when a person became ill. He had the power to communicate with the gods and understand the universe the same as priests. Shamans used rituals

Shamans provided medicines based on their knowledge of illness. They used rituals to tell the meanings of events, foretell the future, and heal the sick.

to try to find the cause of the illness. Part of the cure was to correct the cause of the illness. Often, illness was thought to be caused by harming another person or god. Curing rituals included praying, burning incense, and taking medicines made from local plants.

Midwives

Women took on the job of being **midwives.** A midwife is a woman who helps at the birth of a baby.

In infancy, it was the custom to shape the head of a child into the much-desired flat-forehead look. Boards were placed around a baby's head and bound in place. After a few days, the boards were removed and the baby's head kept the flat-forehead look.

Death

When a person died, the body was wrapped in a shroud. The mouth was filled with maize and a jade bead was also placed in the mouth.

Almost all Maya had flat foreheads—from kings to commoners.

Family Life

Maya families were made up of parents, children, and grandparents. The entire family lived together. Everyone in the household helped with the work.

Men and boys

Men and boys did farm work. They also hunted and fished. They made **basalt** grinding stones and **obsidian** tools. Men were required to give a portion of their time and labor to the community and the king. They helped build and maintain the **temples, causeways,** reservoirs, and other public buildings. In times of war, they served as soldiers.

This woman is grinding corn on a **metate.**

Women and girls

Women and girls made clothes for the family, prepared meals, raised the younger children, and kept a supply of water and firewood in the house. The Maya day began early. Women made breakfast. Men ate and left to work in the fields. At the end of the day, they ate dinner, but the men and women did not eat together.

Methods of weaving have not changed. This present-day Maya woman is using a back strap loom to make cloth. One end is tied to a stick fastened to the wall, the other is attached to a belt around her waist. She can tighten the lengthwise threads by leaning back. Dyed threads are passed back and forth to create patterns.

There were no schools. Children learned skills by observing and helping adults. The wives and mothers of royalty took part in the rituals and duties of Maya kings. Often, women worked as servants and cooks in **noble** and royal households.

Becoming an adult

When children were old enough to be considered adults, the **almanac** was consulted. The **shaman** conducted a coming-of-age ceremony on a day determined by the almanac. A white cloth was placed on each child's head. The shaman said a prayer and gave a bone to the children. The elder tapped each child on the head nine times with the bone. The shaman would then anoint the children with sacred water, and remove the white cloth. Offerings of feathers and **cacao** beans were presented to the shaman by the children. The shaman then cut the white beads from the boys' hair, and the mothers removed the red shells from the girls. After this, the boys and girls were considered adults and eligible to marry.

Men

Since the climate was hot, not much clothing was needed. Men wore loincloths. This was a strip of cloth tied around the hips and passed between the legs. They wore sandals made of untanned deer hide, held to the foot by two thongs. Upper-class people wore clothing made of cotton fabric, with leather belts and sandals. **Nobles** and royalty wore a large square of cotton cloth around the shoulders. Often this was elaborately decorated according to the status of the wearer.

Women

Women wore tunics and skirts, or a loose sleeveless dress that reached the ankles. Upper-class women wore finer clothes decorated with embroidery and ornaments,

These pieces of jade are part of a necklace. They were found in a tomb.

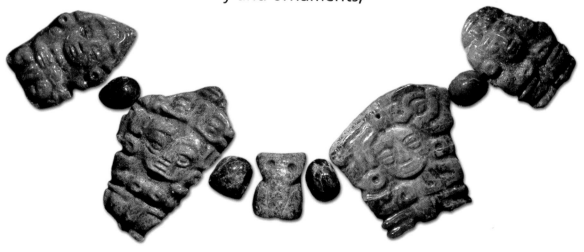

and headdresses made of brightly colored feathers. The wealthy also wore jewelry, carved from green jade and colorful shell.

Jewelry and body art

Everyone wore jewelry. Common people wore simple nose plugs, lip plugs, and earrings of bone, wood, shell, or stone. The elite wore ornaments of jade, stone, **obsidian,** coral, and shell. Some were delicately made **mosaics** and inlays. The elite also wore collars, necklaces, wristlets, anklets, and knee bands. These were made of feathers, jade beads, shells, jaguar teeth and claws, crocodile teeth, and later, gold and copper.

Maya clothing was very colorful. The people that live in the region today still dress in bright styles.

It was considered a mark of beauty to have a flat forehead. Piercing the ears, lips, and nose to hold ornaments was also a mark of beauty. The Maya filed their teeth to make them pointy and put jade in the holes.

Hair

Men wore their hair long, usually braided and wound around the head. Women wore their hair long too, arranged in different ways. Women covered their heads and shoulders with a cotton shawl.

When a baby was born, its parents took it to a priest who predicted its future. Each moment of time was governed by a different god. Thus, the child would serve the particular god who governed the moment of its birth its whole life.

Naming

A boy had three different names during his life. If he was born on the date 7 Ahau of the Mayan calendar, he would first be called Seven Ahau. When he became a young man, he took a new name. He chose his third name when he married. There is no record of how girls received their names.

This girl is feeding corn to her family's chickens. Most Maya children began to work as soon as they were old enough to help.

It is still important to have wood for cooking and building. In Peten, these girls are carrying wood back to their homes.

Maya girls

Girls learned to take care of a family by helping their mothers and other relatives. They learned how to make pottery, prepare food, weave cloth, and make clothes. Women took extra food and crafts to the local markets. In this way, girls learned how to trade and **barter.** Some women became **midwives** or matchmakers.

Maya boys

A Maya boy who was not being trained as a priest, learned from his father how to hunt, trap, fish, and farm. He also learned to make **basalt** grinding tools and **obsidian** cutting tools. As they grew older, boys were expected to give part of their time to help build **temples** and work for the king. Some boys of the elite class learned to become artists, artisans, and **scribes.**

Education

The Maya developed formal education for training nobility and priests. They wanted to preserve their culture, and provide moral and character training.

Living on the Land

Using the land

The Maya depended on the land for everything. They raised many different crops, but they also got fruit and meat from the forests. The rivers and lakes provided fish. Scientists have found net weights made of clay and bone fishhooks. Freshwater fish and mollusks were caught. Along the coast saltwater fish and shellfish were also caught.

Some common forest plants used by the Maya include: papaya, allspice, vanilla, and oregano. Some trees and plants from the forest were also grown in household gardens.

Papaya grew wild in the forests. Maya would often gather the fruit to eat or sell at markets.

Avocadoes were common in the Yucatán Peninsula. Maya would gather this fruit for cooking and trading.

Forests

The forest provided wood for many uses. Firewood was necessary for cooking, firing pottery, and making lime plaster. Hardwoods were used for making houses, furniture, boxes, statues, and other wooden objects. Hardwood was also used for dugout canoes. A dugout canoe is made from one tree. Most wooden items created by the Maya have not survived. The damp, tropical climate caused them to decay.

Other uses of land

Palms, vines, and different fibers were used for rope, sandals, mats, woven baskets, and bark cloth. The resin of the copal tree was shaped into small cakes and burned as incense. The soft material around the seeds of the ceiba, or silk-cotton tree, was used as padding or filling for cushions. This material is called kapok. Many other trees were the source of dyes, medicines, and food.

The Maya called the tropical ceiba tree the "tree of life." They believed it grew from the middle of the earth. They also got kapok fibers from the seed pods of the tree.

The Farming Year

Producing food

Agriculture was the most important means of producing food for the Maya. Some of the most common food plants were amaranth (an herb), avocado, **cacao,** cassava, chili, common bean, guava, maize, papaya, pineapple, squash, sweet potato, and yucca.

Farming techniques

One method the farmers used was called swiddening. After using land for about two or three years, the soil was too poor to grow much, so the farmer had to use another field. He created another field by cutting and burning part of the forest. This is called a slash-and-burn technique, and it is still being used today in some areas.

Rainfall

In the Yucatán Peninsula, the dry season is from January to April. May to December is the rainy season. There is an average of 80–120 inches (203–305 cm) of rainfall a year

This picture shows a farm on the hillside in the Chaipas highlands, where the Maya once farmed.

This farmer sits in his corn grainary during harvest season. The Maya considered maize to be the "sunbeams of the gods."

Over the years, the Maya learned better ways to farm. They learned to build soil platforms that made it possible to farm land that was flooded part of the time. They learned to drain water from low areas. They built canals and irrigated the land in drier regions. In the highlands, they built terraces for their crops.

The rich soil along the riverbanks made it possible to farm almost all year-round. The farmers were able to supply large amounts of maize, beans, and other staples to the large cities. In addition to the farms, each family had its own garden.

Cotton

Cotton was an important crop. Cotton fiber was spun into thread, colored with many different vegetable and mineral dyes, and woven into clothing and textiles.

Maya Homes

Farmers lived in small villages near their fields. Their houses were built of poles tied together with rope. The roofs were made of palm leaves or grass. The space between houses was used for family gardens. Each house could be built in a few days.

Most non-farming families lived in houses made of stone and plaster with **thatched** roofs. Houses sat on plaster pavements supported by large platforms. Each set of homes had its own water tank.

Royal and noble homes

Royalty and **nobles** lived in stone palaces in fortified cities. They controlled most of the wealth and had rights to most of the surrounding land. There were kitchens

Maya farmers would have lived in simple homes like this.

This drawing shows the basic structure of the Maya home. Poles stripped of their bark were set into a stone foundation. Two doorways were placed opposite each other to allow the breeze to flow through. The framework had rounded ends and was filed in with either more poles or **stucco**. A thatch roof sheltered the inside from the weather.

nearby where food was prepared for those who lived in the palace.

A closed courtyard with smaller palaces was grouped around the largest compound. Smaller houses and courtyards were built close to the palaces. These were the homes of the servants and artisans who worked in the palace.

Nobles lived in more spacious homes, sometimes with two stories. Their houses were made of stone.

Burial places

Burial customs were the same for the rich as for the poor. The dead were buried beneath the floors of their houses, or close by. This way, the ancestors stayed close to the family.

Cooking and Eating

Food

The main foods of the Maya diet were maize, beans, and squash. After maize was dried it was ground on a **metate,** or grinding stone. The flour was mixed with water to make a dough. It was formed into flat **tortillas** and baked on a pottery griddle. Sometimes it was wrapped in leaves and steamed in a clay pot to make **tamales.**

Another favorite food of the Maya was the black bean. It was cooked and served whole or mashed and refried. For meat, the Maya hunted deer, rabbit, birds, **peccary, tapir, armadillos,** and monkeys.

These present-day Maya women are making tortillas in the same way their ancestors did.

This Maya grinding table is made of **basalt** and is about 20–25 inches (40–50 cm) long. It was used for grinding grain.

These are some of the bowls and cups that could be found in the average Maya kitchen.

Several kinds of chili were used in cooking, as well as roots such as cassava or manioc. The Maya ate fruits such as avocado, papaya, and guava.

Along the coast, the people caught fish, shellfish, and snails. Dried fish and salt from evaporated seawater were traded at markets.

Beverages

The Maya made a drink called *balche* from fermented honey and the bark of a certain tree. They had other favorite drinks made from maize, honey, and fruits. **Cacao** was used as a drink and sweetened with honey. Chocolate was known as the "drink of the gods."

Sports and Games

Pok-a-tok

Every city had a court where a ball game, called pok-a-tok, was played. This game required skill and endurance. The point of the game was to knock a four-and-a half-pound (two-kilogram) rubber ball through a small ring, using only the elbows, wrists, and hips. This was a serious game with religious meaning. It was symbolic of a myth about the Hero Twins who fought to defeat the death gods. Sometimes the losers were sacrificed.

This figurine shows a pok-a-tok ball player. He is wearing heavy padding around his hips and his wrists.

The elite of society sat on the steps of the surrounding **temples** to watch the game. The rest of the observers stood in the plaza below. Some would be able only to hear the thud of the ball and the cries of those who were able to actually see the game.

Other games

The Maya people worked hard and children had to work early in life, but they probably took some time to play different kinds of ball games. There are accounts carved on stones that give evidence of such games.

In Todos Santos in Guatemala, there is a horse race to celebrate All Saints' Day. The winner is anyone who finishes the race.

A Maya City

Copán

The ancient city of Copán was located on the western side of what is now Honduras. The Copán River twists through this region. Some of the valley has rich land that is good for farming. Other parts of the region are ridges, some as high as 3,000 feet (914 meters). The slopes have ravines that carry rainwater down to the valley.

The people had many different occupations. Some made pottery, others may have been woodworkers. Not much of their work has survived, but many **obsidian** blades have been found. Some people made **metates,** or corn grinders, of **rhyolite.**

Smoke Imix
One of the greatest rulers of Copán was Smoke Imix, who ruled from 628 to 695 C.E. During this time, the city grew and more buildings were erected. Smoke Imix was a great warrior. It was because of his victories that the city grew.

Smoke Imix built an altar in the group of buildings known as the **Acropolis.** On this alter he had his image and the fifteen rulers before him carved. This altar, known as Altar Q, records the entire line of sixteen kings.

The Hieroglyphic Stairway was completed around 755 c.e. by Smoke Shell, who erected the stelae at the foot of the stairs. There are 70 steps to the top of the temple. The steps are carved with more than 2,200 **glyphs.**

The heart of Copán was divided into two sections. On the north was a series of public plazas. In the Middle Plaza, a road from the east met a road from the west. To the north was the Plaza of the **Stelae.** Many fine stelae and altars were there. Most of these were built by a ruler named 18 Rabbit. South from the Middle Plaza was the ball court. Next was the **Hieroglyphic** Stairway, also known as **Temple** 26.

The Acropolis of Copán is about 98 feet (30 meters) at its highest point. It consists of royal palaces and temples built on top of one another over a period of 400 years. Around this area of temples and plazas were the houses where the people lived.

The church and monastery shown here were started in 1553 by Diego de Landa, a Spanish priest. They were built in front of an ancient Maya temple.

Architects and Builders

Gateways and stairways

The Maya did not build many gateways, mostly because they did not put walls around their cities and **temples.** The gate at Labna was built as a showpiece. On either side of the arch are small rooms. Above each room is a balcony. On each side are trellis panels that show how skilled the Maya builders were.

The stairway was the most outstanding achievement of Maya architecture. Both temples and houses were built on platforms raised above ground level. The Maya today still use the same methods for building homes. A framework of poles supports a **thatch** roof. Walls are made from a lattice of sticks plastered with a thick coating of **adobe.**

The Great Gate at Labna, Yucatán, may have been a ceremonial passageway between two plazas.

At the spring equinox on March 21 and the autumn equinox on September 21, the light and shadow strike the edge of this pyramid in such a way that a shadow is formed representing a serpent wriggling down the side to bless the earth.

Building

The building of the temples and palaces was supervised by architects and other specialists. The actual work was done by the common people to fulfill their obligations to the king. Most buildings were made of limestone obtained from quarries. Plaster was used to make a smooth finish on walls, floors, and some roofs.

The walls of the structures had to be very thick in order to support the **corbelled arches** and roofs. This did not leave much space on the inside.

In Tulum, a temple was used as a lighthouse to guide boats through the reef. This was the first Maya structure ever reported by Europeans.

Many buildings were decorated with three-dimensional forms made of **stucco.** Blocks of stone were sculpted and used for **lintels,** wall panels, door posts, and steps.

Crafts and Trades

Many Maya crafts developed out of a household need. Every woman needed cooking pots and vessels to carry water, so she learned to make her own.

Tools and ornaments

Basalt was ground to make chisels, axes, and bark beaters. **Manos** and **metates,** used in every household to grind maize, were made from stone.

The Maya made ornaments from jade. Jade was considered sacred because its blue-green color symbolized the sky and the underworld— the homes of the gods. Working with jade required special skill. Masks and mirrors were made of **mosaics** of jade, **obsidian,** pyrite, turquoise, and shell.

During ancient Maya times, pottery was decorated and traded in markets.

Most Maya wood carvings have not survived in the wet climate. Here is a piece of a wooden **lintel** that has survived from 743 C.E.

Buildings and artwork were often painted with bright colors. Red was the most common color. Mercury was the basis for cinnabar, a red color used in sacred ceremonies. Metals such as copper, silver, and gold were used for jewelry and ritual objects.

Flint and obsidian were chipped to make sharp cutting and scraping tools.

Cloth and fiber

Cotton was grown and woven into cloth. Not many examples have survived. Sculptures and paintings show clothing with complicated weaves and embroidery. Maya women of today continue the tradition of weaving.

Natural fibers were used to make baskets, especially baskets for rough work and carrying corn. Mats were woven of fiber and were considered a mark of importance.

Feathers

Feathers were used to make crest capes, shields, decorations for canopies, fans, and personal ornaments. They also hung from spears and scepters. Feathers were used in fabric and basket embroidery. The scarlet macaw was a common source of feathers. The feathers of the sacred **quetzal** were only used by the king. The quetzal was a symbol of Maya royal power. It can still be found in the remote highland forests.

This mask is made of fuchsite, inlaid with shell and colored with cinnabar. It measures eight inches (twenty cm) high and represents a god of the Palenque underworld.

Buying and Selling

Bartering

The Maya did not use money. Instead, they used a system of **barter,** or exchange. Sometimes they used **cacao** beans for barter, because they had the same value everywhere. They might trade food or clothing for salt or lime.

Markets

Market day was usually one or two days a week. Some market days came at the same time as a special ceremony.

The Maya traded vegetables, fruits, and meat at markets. There were also baskets, rope, pottery, cloth, and brooms available for barter. Even today, farmers grow most of their own food to feed their families. Extra food is then sold at markets.

This man is a present-day merchant at the market in San Cristobal, Mexico. He is selling pineapple.

The markets were probably located in an open plaza with just a pole and **thatch** cover for the stands. Highland capitals may have had permanent plazas for their markets. In the markets, there was a place for government officials to enforce the rules, settle disputes, and collect taxes.

Trade

The Maya traded with people from other cities. This kept them in contact with neighboring cities. The Maya were connected by their commerce.

Another item used for trade was volcanic ash from El Mirador, used to make pottery. **Obsidian,** volcanic stone, and jade were imported in the lowlands. From the lowlands came feathers, animal skins, hardwood, and fibers.

Transportation and Trade

There was much local trading of food and crafts. The Maya also traded with people farther away than their own cities. These traders carried loads of goods on their backs. Packs were slung across a trader's back and carried by using a cord around the pack and forehead. These goods were then sold in other areas.

Roads

Traders carrying goods traveled over limestone roads. Limestone roads connected different parts of a city. They also reached from one city to another. The Maya usually did not use animals to carry loads, and they did not have carts with wheels.

This man is making a dugout canoe from one tree trunk. The Maya had fleets of canoes to carry goods over lakes and rivers and along the seacoasts.

This boy is transporting goods with the help of pack mules.

Trade routes

There were many overland north-south trade routes, but the longest ones were east-west. Some routes covered areas using both land and river transportation. After a time, sea trade became large enough to develop routes around the Yucatán Peninsula. Larger canoes were built that carried more goods and people. One large seagoing canoe could carry more goods and needed fewer people to row it than what could be carried across land.

Columbus meets the Maya

When Christopher Columbus made his fourth voyage across the Atlantic Ocean, he encountered a Maya trading canoe off the coast of present-day Honduras. He described it as being as long as a European galley and eight feet (two meters) wide. It had a cabin in the middle and a crew of about 24 men. There were also women and children on board. It carried a cargo of **cacao,** copper bells, axes, pottery, cotton clothing, and **macanas.**

Weapons and Warfare

Captives

Many of the **hieroglyphic** writings tell stories of Maya rulers who waged war against other Maya cities and took **aristocrats** captive. These captives were usually tortured and sacrificed to the Maya gods. Most of the recorded battles were between neighboring cities. There may have been a sacrifice when a new ruler was put on the throne. Captives were sacrificed during times of celebration or when a new **temple** was built. Sacrificing captives was thought to give the king more power.

Reasons for war

Warfare was the will of the gods. The Maya were not interested in killing. They preferred taking prisoners. Important conflicts between kingdoms were re-enacted in ritual ball games held in the city of the victors. After the game, the losers were sacrificed. These battles were timed to coincide with the position of Venus or with anniversaries of past events. Another reason for war was profit. It increased the wealth and power of one king, while it took away the wealth and power of another.

This captive's hands are tied in front of him and he stands with his head bowed. The text at the side of the figure describes a battle in November 695 C.E.

Maya and the Spanish

When the Spanish first encountered the Maya armies, they found them terrifying. In 1517, Hernandez de Cordoba and his men fought the Maya. The Maya announced their arrival with conch shell trumpets and a terrible whistling noise from the warriors. There was an opening barrage of stones and arrows, followed by rapid hand-to-hand fighting, using lances, shields, and knives. The knives used by the Maya were made of razor-sharp chipped flint.

Warrior dress

Maya warriors were not attractive by today's standards. They were covered with tattoos and body paint and they carried banners. They wore helmets and headdresses, padded cotton armor, and carried shields stretched with animal skin. Their lances were tipped with sharp flint.

Fortifications

Some Maya cities had fortifications. At Calakmul, a large canal circled the center of the city. Tikal was surrounded by man-made embankments made of soil in places where there were no swamps for natural protection.

These Maya projectile points were made from stone and are about 3–4 inches (6–8 cm) long. They were fastened on the end of a lance.

Height of the Maya Civilization

A great civilization

Between 250 and 900 C.E., the Maya culture strengthened and grew. At its peak, the civilization consisted of more than 40 cities. Each city had between 5,000 and 50,000 citizens. The total population was approximately two million people.

Architecture

The Maya were great builders. They built magnificent palaces and lofty pyramids. Even the dwellings of the common people showed skillful engineering and beautiful craftsmanship. Houses in the area today are still made in the same way as the ancient ones.

Writing and surviving artifacts

The Maya writing system was their greatest achievement. Most of the surviving records of

This picture shows an aerial view of Chichén Itzá. The pyramid can be seen at the back right of the image.

The Maya calendar was complicated, but as accurate as the one we use today. They plotted the course of the stars and predicted eclipses of the sun and moon.

historical information is carved on stone monuments, buildings, and **artifacts.** Unfortunately, the books the Maya made of paper decayed over time, due to the wet climate.

Maya artifacts of **mosaic,** jade, and decorated pottery are examples of their artistry. Their textile designs and methods of weaving are still being used today. Unfortunately, the artistic craft of feather work did not survive.

Family values

One of the things that helped the Maya survive was their value of family. They took advantage of the strength of the family and made sure the traditions were passed down from one generation to the next.

This jar has a lid that has to be twisted to remove it. It was found in a tomb.

The Spanish Conquistadores

The Maya were not strangers to trouble. Over the years, they had experienced many bloody wars, natural disasters, and migrations. But they managed to survive.

Spanish dominance

In 1523, the Spanish began to sweep from the Pacific coast to the Guatemalan highlands. The Maya resisted, but the Spanish were too strong. Many Maya died from diseases such as smallpox, measles, and

The Spanish brought packs of vicious hunting dogs and rode into Maya cities on horses.

typhus. The Spanish had weapons and technology that was new to the Maya. They used crossbows and firearms in their conquest. They destroyed the symbols and monuments of Maya gods and the sacred knowledge valued by the Maya for centuries.

The Spanish imposed a system of tribute payment known as the *ecomienda.* Under this system, the Maya were supposed to bring cotton, maize, honey, salt, and turkeys to the Spanish. Another part of this system was the *repartimienti.* This meant the native people were forced to work to build roads, churches, and townhouses for the Spanish foreigners. Many times this meant tearing down the Maya buildings and using the stones to build new ones.

A Catholic priest, Diego de Landa, made his headquarters in Izamal. He built the church and monastery that are still the core of the town. Later, he became a bishop. He burned all the Maya books in order to destroy what he considered uncivilized culture. Only four books survived. Three of them were sent to Europe.

In the southern highlands, Pedro de Alvarado led the first conquest of the Maya.

Decline of the Maya Civilization

Why did the Maya civilization collapse? Why did they stop building large **temples** and pyramids? There are several possible reasons why the Maya civilization declined.

Food shortage

As the population grew, so did the need for food and products. The Maya pattern of farming was to cut the forest, burn the trees and undergrowth, and then plant crops. After a time, the soil becomes worn out and produces less and less. But even with a regular rest period, the soil cannot overcome the damage, and the crops fail. Cutting the forest also causes soil erosion and limits the supply of wood.

Illness and death

From a study of Maya bones, it seems the people became unhealthy and malnourished. When the Spanish arrived and brought new diseases with them, the Maya had no resistance. They died in great numbers and became so weak that the Spanish easily overcame them.

Farmers in the same region today still practice the slash-and-burn methods of the ancient Maya.

The Spanish played a large role in the decline of the Maya civilization. This image shows the Spanish colonization of Tenochtitlan.

More problems

The weather changed—there were more droughts and hurricanes. Trade failures and invasions were other possible reasons. The kings were unable to solve the problems of overpopulation, food shortages, and increasing violence. It is possible the people rebelled against having to work on the great buildings and other structures. These things led to the collapse of powerful Maya rulers.

Many people eventually moved to other areas. In some areas, the politics shifted from the rule of kings to a more democratic government. Unfortunately, much of the information about the rise and fall of the Maya has been lost through the burning of the Maya books by the Spanish.

Spanish Rule

A prophecy

Maya priests foretold that white men with beards would arrive from the ocean and become new gods. When the Spanish arrived, Tutal Xiu, ruler of Uxmal, gave no resistance. The Maya of that region believed the prophecies of the priests and accepted the conquest.

When the Spanish came, they brought disease. There were epidemics of smallpox, measles, and typhus. The Spanish demanded gold and labor from the Maya.

Changes to the Maya civilization

The Spaniards were horrified by the ritual sacrifices of the Maya. They tore down pyramids, broke "idols," and burned the sacred books of the Maya.

The Latin alphabet began to be taught in schools established by the Spanish. The Maya were expected to use the written language of their conquerors.

The Maya worshiped images of **deities** and performed human sacrifice when the Spanish arrived. After they arrived, Christianity was imposed. The public shrines and idols of the

A priest named Diego de Landa described the Maya books as being "full of lies and superstitions of the devil, and we burned them all."

Conquest of the northern Yucatán Peninsula was led by Francisco de Montejo, who got permission from King Charles to conquer the area at his own expense.

Maya were destroyed and public ceremonies were banned. Along with this, much of the Maya learning, including their writing, was lost.

Maya artifacts reach Europe

The Spanish administrators and settlers were not curious about the people they conquered. However, when the **artifacts** of gold ornaments, feather works, textiles, and turquoise-inlaid masks arrived back in Europe, the people there were amazed by what they saw.

Time Line

3114 According to the Maya Long Count, the world is created on August 12 of this year.

2600 Maya civilization begins to form.

2000 Peak of the Olmec civilization.

1500 Start of the Maya Pre-Classic period.

700 Writing is developed in **Mesoamerica.**

400 The earliest known stone solar calendars are used by the Maya. However, stone solar calendars may have been used before this date. Pieces of pottery from this time period are found at Palenque and Ek Balam.

300 The Maya adopt a hierarchical society ruled by **nobles** and kings. The city of Tikal is created.

100 The city of Teotihuacan is founded.

100 The decline of the Olmec civilization.

200 The Classic period starts.

400 The Maya highlands fall to Teotihuacan. Maya culture and language begins to disappear in the highlands.

500 Tikal becomes the first major Maya city.

600 An unknown event destroys Teotihuacan. Tikal becomes the largest Maya city, with a population of more than 500,000 people. The city of Palenque reaches its peak.

683 Pacal dies and is buried in the Temple of **Inscriptions** at Palenque.

738 Copán is conquered by Quiriquá and its king captured.

751 Maya alliances begin to break down. Trade between **city-states** decreases. Conflict between city-states increases.

800 Southern cities go into decline and many are abandoned.

869 Construction in Tikal stops, marking the beginning of the city's decline.

899 Tikal is abandoned.

900 The Classic Period ends with the collapse of the southern lowland cities. Maya cities in the northern Yucatán continue to thrive. The Post-Classic Period begins. The Terminal Classic Period begins and lasts until 1000. This time marks the collapse of the Classic Maya.

976 The Maya tradition gets mixed with the Toltec.

1200 Maya begin to abandon the northern cities. The Dresden **Codex** is written at Chichén Itzá.

1224 Chichén Itzá is abandoned by the Toltecs.

1230 The Grolier Codex is written.

1517 Hernandez de Cordoba arrives on the shores of the Yucatán. The Spanish bring smallpox, influenza, and measles, which kill 90% of Mesoamerica's native population before 1600.

1519 Hernán Cortéz begins exploring the Yucatán.

1524 Cortéz meets the Maya.

1528 The Spanish under Francisco de Montejo begin their conquest of the northern Maya. The Maya fight back, keeping the Spanish away for several years.

1541 The Spanish put an end to Maya resistance.

Glossary

acropolis upper, fortified part of an ancient city

adobe brick or building material made of sun-dried mud and straw

almanac book that contains information on the weather and the stars for a particular year

archaeology study of material remains such as tools, pottery, and writings found from past cultures

aristocrat member of the ruling class or nobility

armadillo animal with an armor of small bony plates. It can curl up into a ball when attacked.

art historian person who studies the history of art

artifact object made by humans

barter to trade goods or services without using money

basalt hard, dense, dark volcanic rock

cacao tropical evergreen American tree. Cacao seed is used in making chocolate, cocoa, and cocoa butter.

causeway raised road across wet ground

city-state politically independent state

codex (more than one are called codices) book

corbelled arch bracket of stone or wood projecting from the face of a wall and used to support an arch

deity god or goddess

epigraphy study of inscriptions

glyph symbol that gives information

hieroglyphic system of writing in which pictures are used to represent words or sounds

inscription letters, numbers, or patterns cut into a solid surface, usually stone

lintel horizontal beam over a window or door that supports the structure above

macana wooden sword with an obsidian blade

mano large stone on which grain is crushed

Mesoamerica region extending south and east from central Mexico to include parts of Guatemala, Belize, Honduras, and Nicaragua

metate corn grinder made of rhyolite, a type of volcanic rock

midwife woman trained to assist in childbirth

mosaic picture or design made by setting small, colored pieces of stone or tile into a surface

noble person born into an important family; a man of noble rank was sometimes called a *nobleman*

obsidian black, shiny volcanic glass

ocarina small wind instrument

peccary Caribbean animal related to the pig

quetzal Central American bird that has bronze-green and red plumage. The male has long, flowing tail feathers.

rhyolite kind of volcanic rock used by the Maya to make metates

sarcophagus stone coffin

scribe person who copies manuscripts; official, public secretary, or clerk

script system of writing

shaman tribal person who acts as a medium between the present world and the spirit world. He practices magic or sorcery for healing.

stela (more than one are called stelae) upright stone or slab inscribed to commemorate an event

stucco combination of cement, sand, and lime applied while wet to walls

tamale mixture of fried, chopped meat and crushed peppers rolled in cornmeal dough and steamed

tapir large animal related to the horse and the rhinoceros

temple place where people worship their gods and goddesses

thatch plant stalks or leaves used as roofing

tortilla thin disc of bread made of corn or wheat flour and baked on a hot surface

vigesimal numbering system based on the number twenty

Xibalba Maya underworld

More Books to Read

Deedrick, Tami. *Maya.* Austin, Tex.: Raintree Steck-Vaughn, 2001.

Mason, Antony. *Ancient Civilizations of the Americas.* New York: Dorling Kindersley, 2001.

Netzley, Patricia D. *Mayan Civilization.* Farmington Hills, Mich.: Gale Group, 2002.

Index